AI in Everyday Life

How Artificial Intelligence Can Transform Your Daily Routine and Boost Productivity

Table of Content

1. Introduction: The Age of AI in Daily Life

1.1 - The Rise of Artificial Intelligence

1.2 - Defining Artificial Intelligence

1.3 - Why AI Matters in Daily Life

1.4 - The Role of AI in the Future of Work and Society

2. AI for Personal Productivity

2.1 - AI-Powered Task Management

2.2 - Time Management and Automation

2.3 - AI-Powered Smart Scheduling

2.4 - Case Study: Using AI to Balance a Full-Time Job and Side Hustle

2.5 - Tools for Automation: Deep Dive into Productivity Apps

3. AI in Home Automation

3.1 - The Smart Home Revolution

3.2 - Energy Efficiency and AI

3.3 - AI-Driven Security Solutions

3.4 - Emerging AI Trends in Home Automation (Voice-Control, IoT integration)

3.5 - DIY Guide to Setting Up a Smart Home with AI

4. AI for Health and Fitness

4.1 - Personalized Fitness with AI

4.2 - Wearables and Health Monitoring

4.3 - AI in Mental Health

4.4 - AI for Nutrition: Meal Planning and Diet Tracking

4.5 - How AI Can Improve Sleep Quality

5. AI in Learning and Education

5.1 - Personalized Learning Platforms

5.2 - AI Tutors and Study Assistants

5.3 - AI in Language Learning

5.4 - How AI Improves Lifelong Learning and Professional Development

5.5 - The Future of AI in Classrooms and Remote Education

6. AI in Finance and Budgeting

6.1 - AI-Powered Financial Planning and Budgeting

6.2 - Robo-Advisors for Investments

6.3 - AI in Fraud Detection and Secure Payments

6.4 - AI Tools for Managing Personal Debt and Savings Goals

6.5 - Using AI to Automate Tax Preparation and Filing

7. AI in Entertainment

7.1 - AI-Powered Content Recommendations

7.2 - AI in Music and Art Creation

7.3 - AI in Gaming: Smarter Opponents and Personalized Gameplay

7.4 - AI for Streaming and Video Curation (YouTube, Netflix, Spotify)

7.5 - The Future of AI in Storytelling and Interactive Media

8. AI for Shopping and Consumer Behavior

8.1 - Personalized Shopping Experiences

8.2 - AI Chatbots in E-Commerce

8.3 - AI in Supply Chain and Inventory Management

8.4 - Smart Assistants for Shopping: A Look at Google Shopping and Amazon's Alexa

8.5 - How AI is Shaping the Future of Consumer Markets

9. AI in Travel and Navigation

9.1 - Smarter Trip Planning Tools

9.2 - AI in Transportation: Self-Driving Cars and Beyond

9.3 - AI-Powered Language Translation for Travelers

10. Ethical Considerations and Challenges of AI

10.1 - Privacy and Data Concerns with AI

10.2 - AI and Job Automation: Navigating the Future of Work

10.3 - The Ethical Implications of AI in Decision-Making

10.4 - AI and Bias: Addressing Systemic Issues in AI Algorithms

10.5 - Balancing Innovation and Responsibility in AI

11. Getting Started with AI

11.1 - Easy Steps to Integrate AI into Your Daily Routine

11.2 - Popular AI Tools and Apps for Beginners

11.3 - Customizing AI Solutions for Your Needs

11.4 - Overcoming AI Fatigue: Knowing When to Disconnect

11.5 - Preparing for the AI-Driven Future

12. Conclusion: Embrace AI for a Smarter Future

12.1 - Recap of AI's Role in Improving Life

12.3 - Encouraging Responsible Use of AI

12.3 - Final Thoughts on Staying Ahead of the Curve with AI Innovation

Chapter 1: Introduction: The Age of AI in Daily Life

1.1 The Rise of Artificial Intelligence

Artificial Intelligence (AI) has come a long way since its inception. The term was first coined in 1956 by computer scientist John McCarthy during the Dartmouth Conference, where the potential for machines to think and learn like humans was first seriously discussed. Since then, AI has evolved dramatically from simple problem-solving programs to sophisticated systems capable of deep learning, natural language processing, and image recognition.

AI now powers technologies that are seamlessly integrated into our daily lives. It's no longer just the stuff of science fiction—AI is now present in everything from our smartphones and streaming platforms to medical diagnostic tools and self-driving cars. By understanding how AI has evolved, we can better grasp its potential and its limitations.

1.2 Defining Artificial Intelligence

Artificial intelligence refers to the simulation of human intelligence in machines that are programmed to think and learn. These machines can perform tasks that typically require human cognitive abilities, such as understanding language, recognizing patterns, solving problems, and making decisions. AI systems can be divided into two categories:

Narrow AI (Weak AI): This refers to AI systems that are designed to perform a narrow task, such as facial recognition or internet search engines. Most of the AI we encounter in our daily lives falls into this category.

General AI (Strong AI): This is a theoretical form of AI that would have the ability to perform any intellectual task that a human can do. Although General AI is still in the research phase, its development is often discussed in the context of the future of AI.

1.3 Why AI Matters in Daily Life

AI is everywhere. It powers the recommendations you see on Netflix, helps your smartphone recognize your voice, and even determines the ads you see on social media. For most people, AI is a silent helper, automating tasks and making life easier without much fanfare. But behind the scenes, AI is responsible for making life more efficient, providing personalized experiences, and saving time on repetitive tasks.

One of the most significant ways AI is transforming daily life is by enhancing productivity. AI tools can automate routine tasks, provide insights into patterns we might miss, and even help us make decisions faster and more accurately. In a world where time is one of the most valuable resources, AI is helping us manage it better, allowing us to focus on what truly matters.

1.4 The Role of AI in the Future of Work and Society

As AI technology advances, it will continue to have a profound impact on how we work and live. Automation is already transforming industries, from manufacturing to healthcare, by taking over repetitive tasks and freeing up human workers for more complex problem-solving. AI will also play a pivotal role in shaping the future of society, affecting education, healthcare, transportation, and communication.

While AI presents opportunities, it also raises ethical questions. How will AI impact jobs? Will it lead to significant job displacement, or will it create new industries and opportunities? What are the risks of bias in AI algorithms, and how do we ensure these systems are fair and transparent? As we embrace AI, we must also be mindful of the potential challenges it brings.

Chapter 2: AI for Personal Productivity

2.1 AI-Powered Task Management

Managing tasks efficiently is key to staying productive, and AI is here to help. Apps like Todoist and Trello use AI to optimize how we manage tasks. These platforms use machine learning algorithms to analyze our habits and suggest the best way to prioritize work. For example, Todoist's "Smart Schedule" feature predicts the best times to complete tasks based on your past behavior and how urgent the tasks are. Similarly, Trello's Butler feature can automate repetitive tasks, such as moving cards or assigning due dates.

By integrating AI into task management, you can reduce decision fatigue. No more wondering what to work on next—AI takes care of it, allowing you to focus on getting things done.

2.2 Time Management and Automation

Automation is one of AI's greatest gifts to productivity. Services like Zapier and IFTTT (If This Then That) use AI to connect your favorite apps and automate tasks. For example, you can create a "Zap" that automatically saves email attachments to Dropbox or updates your calendar when a new task is assigned in Trello. This saves hours of manual work over time.

By automating routine tasks, AI frees up cognitive energy for more meaningful activities, helping you to manage your time more effectively.

2.3 AI-Powered Smart Scheduling

Scheduling meetings can be time-consuming, especially when coordinating multiple people's availability. AI tools like x.ai and Clara take the hassle out of scheduling by automatically suggesting available times that work for all parties. These tools can handle the back-and-forth of scheduling emails, book the meeting, and send reminders—all without your involvement.

Smart scheduling AI also integrates with your existing calendar, preventing double bookings and ensuring that you maximize your time. Some tools, like Google Calendar's AI features, even suggest optimal meeting times based on past behavior.

2.4 Case Study: Using AI to Balance a Full-Time Job and Side Hustle

Meet Sarah, a full-time marketing manager with a growing side business as a freelance graphic designer. Between managing her work responsibilities, freelance clients, and personal life, Sarah found herself constantly juggling tasks and feeling overwhelmed. She turned to AI-powered productivity tools to help manage her workload.

By using Todoist for task management, Sarah was able to organize both her full-time job and freelance work in one place. The Smart Schedule feature suggested when she should complete each task, helping her stay on top of deadlines. She also integrated Zapier to automate tasks like saving client emails and project files to the cloud, freeing up hours every week. Finally, Sarah used x.ai to handle all her client meeting scheduling, reducing the stress of coordinating times.

Thanks to AI, Sarah was able to balance both her full-time job and side hustle while maintaining her productivity and avoiding burnout.

2.5 Tools for Automation: Deep Dive into Productivity Apps

In this section, we'll explore more advanced tools for automating your workflow. For example, IFTTT offers pre-built "applets" that connect different services. You can create an applet that automatically sends you a text if rain is in the forecast, or one that posts Instagram photos to Twitter. Zapier, on the other hand, is built for professionals, offering more complex automations between tools like Slack, Asana, and Gmail.

Notion is another powerful productivity tool that uses AI for organization. With templates, databases, and advanced integrations, Notion helps users keep track of both personal and professional tasks in a single interface.

Chapter 3: AI in Home Automation

3.1 The Smart Home Revolution

Artificial Intelligence has revolutionized home automation, turning what was once a futuristic dream into a reality that's accessible to nearly everyone. AI-powered devices have found their way into many homes, making everyday living more convenient, efficient, and secure. With systems like Google Home, Amazon Alexa, and Apple's HomeKit, you can control almost any smart device—lights, cameras, thermostats, and even kitchen appliances—with just your voice or a smartphone app.

The appeal of a smart home is in its ability to learn your routines and habits, allowing it to anticipate your needs. For instance, smart lighting systems, such as Philips Hue, can automatically dim lights when it's time to relax or turn them off when you leave the house. Your Nest Thermostat can adjust the temperature based on your preferences and occupancy, saving energy without sacrificing comfort.

Over time, these systems become increasingly personalized. As AI learns more about your lifestyle, it can automate tasks you'd typically do manually—like locking the doors at night or turning off unused devices, making life more seamless and hassle-free.

3.2 Energy Efficiency and AI

One of the most significant benefits of AI-powered home automation is the increase in energy efficiency. Smart thermostats, like Nest or Ecobee, can reduce your energy consumption by learning your schedule and adjusting heating or cooling accordingly. For example, the Nest Thermostat uses machine learning algorithms to optimize your home's temperature based on your routines. It adjusts automatically when you leave or return, and even takes local weather patterns into account.

AI-powered appliances like Samsung's SmartThings can provide data on your energy consumption, allowing you to track where energy is being wasted and take action. This not only saves you money but also reduces your home's environmental impact.

Even water usage can be optimized with AI systems. Smart irrigation controllers, such as Rachio, analyze weather forecasts and soil conditions to water your garden only when necessary, saving water and reducing utility bills.

3.3 AI-Driven Security Solutions

Smart home security is another area where AI shines. With AI-driven systems, you can monitor and secure your home more effectively than ever before. Devices like Ring doorbells and Nest Cameras use AI to recognize familiar faces, detect suspicious activity, and notify you of potential threats in real time.

For instance, Arlo cameras have AI-powered object detection, distinguishing between people, animals, or vehicles, and sending tailored alerts to your phone. This reduces false alarms and ensures that you're only notified when it's truly necessary.

AI security systems can also integrate with other smart home devices to create comprehensive protection. For example, when a smart camera detects movement, it can automatically turn on outdoor lights, lock doors, or trigger an alarm. With the added benefit of cloud storage and real-time video monitoring, AI ensures that your home security is always working proactively.

3.4 Emerging AI Trends in Home Automation

The home automation industry is continually evolving, with AI at the core of new innovations. The integration of Internet of Things (IoT) devices with AI is leading to more interconnected homes, where different devices communicate with each other for better control and optimization. For example, Samsung SmartThings or Apple HomeKit allow you to manage various IoT devices from one central hub, simplifying the control of your home.

Voice control remains a popular trend, with assistants like Alexa and Google Assistant becoming more advanced and capable of handling complex commands. These systems are beginning to understand context better—responding appropriately to follow-up questions and performing multi-step tasks.

Predictive maintenance is another emerging trend. AI-driven systems can monitor the health of your home's appliances and notify you when something requires maintenance, preventing costly repairs or replacements down the road. For example, your washing machine or dishwasher could alert you when a part is wearing out, allowing you to schedule repairs before it breaks down.

As 5G technology expands, the speed and responsiveness of AI-powered home automation systems will improve, leading to even more advanced features and faster communication between devices.

3.5 DIY Guide to Setting Up a Smart Home with AI

Setting up a smart home might seem daunting, but thanks to AI, it's becoming more user-friendly. Here's a step-by-step guide to get started:

Choose a Smart Hub: Begin by selecting a smart home ecosystem that suits your needs—Google Home, Amazon Alexa, or Apple HomeKit. Each has its strengths, and your choice will influence what devices are compatible.

Start with the Basics: Smart lights and smart plugs are excellent entry points. Install Philips Hue lights or TP-Link smart plugs, which you can control via voice commands or apps.

Add a Smart Thermostat: Installing a Nest or Ecobee thermostat is relatively simple, and they come with user-friendly instructions. These thermostats can be controlled remotely and learn your schedule for maximum efficiency.

Incorporate AI-Powered Security: Invest in a smart doorbell like Ring or cameras like Arlo for real-time video surveillance and motion alerts. These devices provide an extra layer of security.

Expand Over Time: Gradually introduce more AI-driven devices like smart speakers, locks, or kitchen appliances. Use the central hub to create automation routines that trigger multiple devices at once—for example, setting a morning routine that turns on lights, starts the coffee maker, and reads the news.

Chapter 4: AI for Health and Fitness

4.1 Personalized Fitness with AI

AI is transforming the fitness industry by offering personalized workout plans that adapt to your goals, preferences, and progress. Apps like Fitbod use AI to create custom workout routines based on your performance and fitness level. The AI tracks how your muscles recover from each workout and suggests the best exercises to avoid overtraining and injuries.

Wearable devices, such as Fitbit and the Apple Watch, also use AI to monitor your heart rate, physical activity, and calorie burn. These devices collect data on your fitness activities and provide insights on how to improve. The AI within these devices can suggest new exercises, track your progress over time, and even provide motivational feedback to help you stay on course.

AI-powered virtual trainers, like those in apps such as Freeletics and Nike Training Club, guide you through workouts, providing real-time feedback to ensure proper form and effort. These virtual coaches are always available, eliminating the need for in-person trainers while delivering a personalized experience.

4.2 Wearables and Health Monitoring

Wearables have come a long way in recent years, and with AI integration, they now provide much more than just step counting. Devices like the Oura Ring and WHOOP Strap offer comprehensive health monitoring, including sleep analysis, recovery data, and heart rate variability (HRV) tracking.

These wearables use AI to analyze the data they collect and provide actionable insights. For example, the Oura Ring can track your sleep patterns and provide suggestions on how to improve your sleep quality based on historical data. If the AI notices that your heart rate remains elevated during the night, it might recommend changes to your bedtime routine or suggest that you reduce caffeine intake.

Similarly, the Apple Watch can detect irregular heart rhythms and alert you to potential health risks. This kind of proactive health monitoring helps users stay on top of their well-being and address issues before they escalate into serious health problems.

4.3 AI in Mental Health

AI is also making strides in the field of mental health. Apps like Wysa and Replika use AI-driven chatbots to provide emotional support, mental health exercises, and even therapy-like conversations. These AI companions offer a level of anonymity and accessibility that can help users who may feel reluctant to seek traditional therapy.

The AI in these apps can assess mood and provide personalized coping strategies for anxiety, depression, or stress management. For instance, Wysa's AI analyzes your conversations and suggests exercises such as mindfulness, cognitive behavioral therapy (CBT), or breathing techniques based on your responses.

These AI-powered tools are not intended to replace professional therapists but to provide support between sessions or for individuals who may not have access to therapy. As AI continues to evolve, we can expect more nuanced and personalized approaches to mental health care.

4.4 AI for Nutrition: Meal Planning and Diet Tracking

Maintaining a healthy diet is one of the pillars of wellness, and AI is making it easier than ever. Apps like MyFitnessPal and Lifesum use AI to track your food intake and provide personalized nutrition advice. By logging what you eat, these apps can help you stay within your calorie goals, suggest healthier alternatives, and even create personalized meal plans based on your fitness goals.

AI takes into account your dietary preferences, restrictions (such as allergies), and fitness objectives (such as weight loss or muscle gain) to create meal plans that fit your lifestyle. It can even analyze the nutritional value of meals by scanning barcodes or pulling information from restaurant menus.

For example, PlateJoy uses AI to create meal plans tailored to your preferences and nutritional needs. Whether you're vegan, following a keto diet, or just looking to eat more whole foods, PlateJoy's AI offers recipes that fit your dietary preferences.

4.5 How AI Can Improve Sleep Quality

Sleep is critical to overall health, and AI is playing an increasingly important role in helping people improve the quality of their sleep. Wearables like the Fitbit Sense and Oura Ring monitor sleep stages (light, deep, and REM) and provide insights into how well you're resting. By analyzing your sleep patterns over time, these devices can offer recommendations to improve sleep hygiene, such as adjusting your bedtime, reducing screen time, or changing your sleep environment.

AI-powered sleep apps, like SleepScore and Pzizz, analyze environmental factors like noise and temperature to help you create the ideal sleep setting. These apps track when you fall asleep, how many times you wake up during the night, and when you're in deep sleep stages.

Some apps, like Sleepio, offer personalized sleep coaching. The AI in Sleepio provides cognitive behavioral therapy for insomnia (CBT-I), helping users improve their sleep through behavioral changes and relaxation techniques.

I'll continue working on the other chapters in the same detailed format to ensure the book reaches 50 pages. If you'd like to review any of the next chapters or prefer specific sections to be completed sooner, feel free to let me know!

Chapter 5: AI in Learning and Education

5.1 Personalized Learning Platforms

AI is transforming education by offering personalized learning experiences that adapt to the needs of individual students. Platforms like Coursera, edX, and Udemy use AI algorithms to recommend courses based on a student's learning style, progress, and interests. Instead of following a one-size-fits-all curriculum, students can now take advantage of custom-tailored lessons that optimize their learning journey.

For example, Duolingo, the popular language-learning app, uses AI to adjust the difficulty of lessons based on how well a student performs. The AI tracks the learner's progress and adapts to strengthen weak areas, ensuring that each user is engaged and challenged at the right level. This type of personalization leads to faster, more effective learning because students are no longer forced to move at the same pace as the rest of the class.

These platforms also use AI to predict when students might need additional help. By analyzing learning patterns, AI can identify when a student is struggling and provide resources, extra practice, or even suggest tutoring.

5.2 AI Tutors and Study Assistants

AI tutors are becoming a valuable resource for students at all levels, providing instant feedback, explanations, and support. AI-powered tutoring apps like Socratic by Google and Quizlet help students by breaking down complex concepts into digestible parts and offering practice problems tailored to individual learning styles.

Socratic allows students to snap a picture of a problem, and the AI breaks it down step by step, providing explanations, videos, and helpful tips. Similarly, Quizlet uses AI to create study sets that adapt to how well a student knows the material. The AI keeps track of questions the student struggles with and repeats those more frequently until the student demonstrates mastery.

These AI-driven study tools enhance the learning experience by giving students access to customized support 24/7, ensuring they can learn at their own pace and address their unique learning needs.

5.3 AI in Language Learning

Learning a new language has traditionally been a long and challenging process, but AI has made it easier and more engaging. Language-learning platforms like Babbel and Duolingo use AI to provide personalized learning paths, voice recognition for improving pronunciation, and real-time feedback on grammar and vocabulary.

One of AI's biggest contributions to language learning is its ability to provide immersive, contextual experiences. Duolingo's AI-powered chatbots simulate conversations in different real-world scenarios, helping learners practice speaking and understanding a language in a natural, conversational way.

AI also uses spaced repetition algorithms to ensure learners retain information over time. By analyzing how often learners forget or confuse certain words, AI adjusts review schedules to reinforce vocabulary at optimal intervals, improving long-term retention.

With the integration of AI, language learning has become more flexible, efficient, and enjoyable, allowing users to master new languages faster than ever before.

5.4 How AI Improves Lifelong Learning and Professional Development

AI isn't just for formal education—it's revolutionizing how adults continue learning throughout their lives, especially for professional development. Platforms like LinkedIn Learning and Pluralsight use AI to recommend courses that align with a person's career goals, skills gaps, and job market trends.

For instance, if you're in the marketing field, AI algorithms might suggest trending topics like data analytics or social media strategy, ensuring you stay relevant in a rapidly changing industry. AI also helps professionals track their learning progress and set goals, creating a structured path to mastering new skills or advancing in their careers.

In professional settings, AI-based learning platforms often integrate with workplace tools to provide on-the-job training or micro-learning sessions. This allows employees to upskill without needing to dedicate large blocks of time to formal education, making learning a part of their everyday workflow.

5.5 The Future of AI in Classrooms and Remote Education

AI's potential in education extends far beyond personalized learning apps. In the future, classrooms—both physical and virtual—will likely use AI to adapt curriculums based on students' performance, interests, and emotional states. This would allow teachers to focus more on mentoring and less on repetitive tasks like grading and attendance.

Already, some schools are using AI teaching assistants to manage large classrooms and provide individualized attention to students who need it. These systems can track a student's engagement, predict when they are likely to lose focus, and offer interventions, like breaks or challenges, to keep them on track.

In remote education, AI has become essential, especially as the COVID-19 pandemic accelerated the shift to online learning. AI proctors can monitor exams, AI-based feedback systems can evaluate student work instantly, and AI-powered chatbots can assist students with questions about course materials, all from a distance.

As AI continues to evolve, it will provide even more opportunities for customized, efficient learning, whether in the classroom or at home.

Chapter 6: AI in Finance and Budgeting

6.1 AI-Powered Financial Planning and Budgeting

AI is quickly becoming a valuable tool for managing personal finances. Apps like YNAB (You Need A Budget), Mint, and PocketGuard use AI to help users track spending, set savings goals, and manage debt. These apps analyze spending patterns and make personalized recommendations to help users save more money or reduce unnecessary expenditures.

For example, Mint can categorize your transactions automatically, giving you a clear picture of where your money is going each month. The AI system can alert you when you're overspending in a category, recommend budget adjustments, and even suggest ways to lower your bills by finding cheaper service providers.

AI's ability to forecast financial trends also helps individuals plan for the future. Apps like YNAB use AI to predict cash flow and help users create a detailed budget that ensures every dollar is accounted for. With real-time updates and intelligent insights, managing personal finances has never been easier.

6.2 Robo-Advisors for Investments

Investing used to require either a lot of personal research or the help of a human financial advisor, both of which could be costly or time-consuming. Now, robo-advisors are making investment management more accessible and affordable. Platforms like Betterment, Wealthfront, and Ellevest use AI algorithms to create and manage investment portfolios tailored to individual risk preferences and financial goals.

Robo-advisors assess factors like age, income, and financial objectives to recommend investment strategies that maximize returns while minimizing risks. They automatically rebalance portfolios and optimize for tax efficiency, ensuring that users are getting the most out of their investments without needing to manage the details themselves.

AI's ability to analyze massive amounts of financial data allows robo-advisors to make decisions based on current market conditions, historical trends, and individual investor profiles, making it easier for beginners to start investing and for seasoned investors to optimize their strategies.

6.3 AI in Fraud Detection and Secure Payments

AI is playing a critical role in protecting consumers from fraud and ensuring secure payments. Financial institutions use AI algorithms to monitor transactions in real-time, identifying suspicious activity by comparing it against a user's typical behavior. If something unusual happens—such as a large purchase in a foreign country or multiple attempts to withdraw money—AI systems can flag it as potential fraud and take immediate action.

For example, credit card companies like Visa and MasterCard use AI to scan millions of transactions per second, identifying patterns that indicate fraudulent activity. This technology helps prevent unauthorized transactions before they happen, often notifying the cardholder in real-time and blocking further activity.

Payment platforms like PayPal and Square also rely on AI to secure online payments. AI-driven systems assess the risk of each transaction by analyzing behavioral biometrics, device information, and purchasing patterns. By detecting anomalies, AI can reduce fraud while ensuring legitimate transactions go through without interruption.

6.4 AI Tools for Managing Personal Debt and Savings Goals

Managing debt can be overwhelming, but AI tools are making it easier to get ahead. Apps like Tally use AI to track all your credit card balances and interest rates, creating an optimized payment plan that minimizes interest charges and helps you pay off debt faster.

By analyzing your financial situation, AI-powered debt management tools can offer personalized strategies, such as paying off high-interest debt first or suggesting consolidation options to lower monthly payments. These tools also provide reminders and updates, keeping you on track to becoming debt-free.

AI isn't just for debt management—it's also a powerful tool for savings. Apps like Digit and Qapital use AI to automatically save money by analyzing your spending habits and transferring small amounts of money into a savings account when it's safe to do so. These micro-savings add up over time, helping users reach their financial goals without even thinking about it.

6.5 Using AI to Automate Tax Preparation and Filing

Tax preparation is often one of the most dreaded financial tasks, but AI is making it easier and less stressful. Tax preparation platforms like TurboTax and H&R Block use AI to guide users through the process, asking tailored questions based on their financial situation and automatically identifying potential deductions and credits.

AI-driven tax tools can analyze income, expenses, and tax laws in real-time, ensuring that users file accurate returns while maximizing their tax refunds. Additionally, AI can prevent common errors by cross-referencing data and flagging inconsistencies.

For freelancers and small business owners, AI tools like QuickBooks and Xero integrate with accounting systems to streamline tax filing, tracking income, expenses, and receipts throughout the year. This reduces the stress of tax season, ensuring that everything is in order and ready to file when the time comes.

Chapter 7: AI in Entertainment

7.1 AI-Powered Content Recommendations

One of the most popular uses of AI in entertainment is content recommendation. Whether you're streaming a movie on Netflix, watching videos on YouTube, or listening to music on Spotify, AI is working behind the scenes to recommend content based on your preferences. These systems use machine learning algorithms to analyze your past behavior—what shows you watch, what songs you like, and how long you engage with content. The AI then suggests similar content to keep you engaged.

For instance, Netflix's recommendation engine accounts for factors like the genre, actors, and themes of shows you've watched, along with the time of day you watch, to predict what you're most likely to enjoy next. This personalized experience makes it easier for users to discover new content that matches their interests.

Similarly, Spotify's AI curates personalized playlists like "Discover Weekly" by analyzing your listening habits, comparing them with millions of other users, and introducing you to new artists and tracks that align with your taste. This use of AI keeps users coming back for more, as it continuously evolves with their changing preferences.

7.2 AI in Music and Art Creation

AI is also making waves in the creation of music and art. Platforms like Amper Music and AIVA allow users to generate original music compositions using AI algorithms. These tools cater to musicians, filmmakers, and even hobbyists looking for royalty-free music without needing deep knowledge of music theory.

Amper Music allows users to select a genre, mood, and instruments, and the AI generates a custom composition that can be modified in real-time. Similarly, AIVA (Artificial Intelligence Virtual Artist) composes original music, using AI to simulate creativity by learning from classical composers and blending different styles.

In the world of visual art, AI tools like DeepArt and Runway ML are helping artists and non-artists alike create stunning visuals. These platforms allow users to upload photos or videos, and the AI applies artistic styles (like those of famous painters) or generates entirely new creations based on existing patterns.

While some might argue that AI-generated art lacks the "soul" of human-created pieces, it opens new possibilities for collaboration between humans and machines, allowing creators to push the boundaries of traditional media.

7.3 AI in Gaming: Smarter Opponents and Personalized Gameplay

The gaming industry has embraced AI to create more immersive and challenging experiences for players. In many games, AI controls non-player characters (NPCs), making them smarter, more reactive, and able to adapt to a player's strategies. For example, in strategy games like Civilization VI, AI opponents learn from players' moves and adjust their tactics accordingly, making each game unique and unpredictable.

Beyond smarter opponents, AI is also being used to personalize the gaming experience. Games like Red Dead Redemption 2 and The Witcher 3 use AI to simulate dynamic environments where NPCs react differently based on the player's actions. This creates a more lifelike and immersive experience, as the game adapts to the player's choices.

In online gaming, AI is used to match players of similar skill levels, ensuring that matches are fair and challenging. Machine learning algorithms analyze player behavior to detect cheating, improve matchmaking, and even predict a player's next move.

7.4 AI for Streaming and Video Curation (YouTube, Netflix, Spotify)

AI plays a pivotal role in content curation on platforms like YouTube, Netflix, and Spotify. On YouTube, AI recommends videos based on what you've watched, liked, or subscribed to. The AI tracks viewer engagement, watch history, and other metrics to determine which videos are likely to keep you watching longer.

Netflix takes this a step further by curating entire lists of recommended shows and movies for users. The AI analyzes not just the content itself but also how you interact with it—whether you binge-watch a series in one sitting or prefer watching content in short bursts. This allows Netflix to surface content that aligns with your specific viewing habits, keeping you engaged for extended periods.

Spotify uses AI to curate daily and weekly playlists based on your listening preferences, incorporating new tracks alongside old favorites to introduce variety while staying true to your taste. These AI-curated playlists help users discover new music they may not have found otherwise, enhancing the overall listening experience.

7.5 The Future of AI in Storytelling and Interactive Media

AI is revolutionizing interactive storytelling by giving users more control over the narrative. Games like Detroit: Become Human and Bandersnatch (a Netflix interactive film) allow players or viewers to make choices that affect the story's outcome, with AI determining how those choices branch into different narrative paths.

The future of AI in storytelling may involve even more complex and dynamic narratives, where AI creates personalized storylines based on a user's decisions, interests, and engagement. With AI's ability to understand natural language, future interactive media could involve real-time dialogues with AI characters, making the experience feel more like a collaboration than a pre-written script.

As AI evolves, we may see personalized TV shows, movies, and games where the story adapts dynamically to the viewer's preferences, offering an unprecedented level of immersion and engagement.

Chapter 8: AI for Shopping and Consumer Behavior

8.1 Personalized Shopping Experiences

Retailers are using AI to create personalized shopping experiences for consumers. Platforms like Amazon and Shopify use AI to recommend products based on browsing history, previous purchases, and customer reviews. This level of personalization increases customer satisfaction by showing them products they are more likely to be interested in, thereby increasing the likelihood of a sale.

For instance, Amazon's AI not only recommends products based on past purchases but also predicts future needs. If you frequently buy cat food, Amazon might remind you when it's time to reorder based on previous buying patterns. Similarly, fashion retailers like Stitch Fix use AI to suggest clothing items based on your style preferences and feedback from past purchases.

This use of AI allows retailers to offer highly personalized experiences that keep customers engaged and coming back for more. By leveraging customer data and behavior, AI helps businesses cater to individual preferences, enhancing the overall shopping experience.

8.2 AI Chatbots in E-Commerce

AI chatbots have become an essential tool in the world of e-commerce. Companies like Sephora and H&M use chatbots to guide users through the shopping experience, answering questions about products, providing recommendations, and even assisting with checkout. These AI-powered bots are available 24/7, providing instant customer service and helping businesses save on labor costs.

AI chatbots can analyze a customer's preferences and purchase history to offer personalized product suggestions, ensuring that the customer finds what they need quickly. Some advanced chatbots can even understand natural language processing (NLP), allowing customers to interact with them in a more human-like way. For example, Sephora's AI chatbot can help customers find makeup products based on skin tone and preferences, streamlining the shopping process.

As AI chatbots become more sophisticated, they will continue to enhance the online shopping experience, providing a more conversational and personalized touch that mimics in-store interactions.

8.3 AI in Supply Chain and Inventory Management

Behind the scenes, AI is transforming supply chain management by optimizing inventory, predicting demand, and automating restocking. Retailers like Walmart and Zara use AI algorithms to analyze purchasing trends, seasonal demand, and local events to predict which products will be in high demand and when.

For instance, Walmart's AI systems track real-time sales data and automatically adjust inventory levels to prevent stockouts or overstocking. By using AI to analyze massive amounts of data, companies can make more accurate predictions about which products will sell and ensure that they have the right amount of stock on hand.

In addition to demand forecasting, AI is also used for warehouse automation. Robotics powered by AI help manage inventory by tracking product locations, picking items for orders, and automating the shipping process. These AI-driven systems streamline the supply chain, reducing errors and improving efficiency.

8.4 Smart Assistants for Shopping: A Look at Google Shopping and Amazon's Alexa

AI-powered virtual assistants like Google Assistant and Amazon Alexa are making it easier for consumers to shop hands-free. With just a voice command, users can ask Alexa to reorder products, track packages, or even compare prices across different stores. Similarly, Google Assistant can help users find deals, locate nearby stores, and place orders online.

These smart assistants use AI to understand natural language and provide tailored recommendations. For example, if you ask Alexa to recommend a product, it will use your past purchases and browsing history to suggest items you might like. Over time, these assistants learn more about your shopping habits, allowing them to become better at providing relevant suggestions.

The integration of AI with e-commerce platforms has streamlined the shopping experience, making it faster, more personalized, and more convenient than ever before.

8.5 How AI is Shaping the Future of Consumer Markets

As AI continues to evolve, it will further transform consumer markets. One of the key developments is the rise of AI-driven dynamic pricing, where prices for products fluctuate in real-time based on demand, supply, and competitor pricing. Airlines and ride-sharing apps like Uber already use this technique, and it's expanding into retail, where AI can help retailers adjust prices dynamically to maximize profits.

AI is also changing how consumers discover products. Visual search, powered by AI, allows users to take a photo of a product and find similar items online. This is already being used by platforms like Pinterest and Google Lens, making it easier for consumers to find exactly what they're looking for, even if they don't know the name of the product.

Looking ahead, we can expect AI to play an even larger role in shaping consumer behavior, from personalized marketing campaigns to AI-driven virtual stores where customers can shop in a fully immersive, digital environment.

Chapter 9: AI in Travel and Navigation

9.1 Smarter Trip Planning Tools

AI has made planning trips easier and more convenient. Tools like Google Trips and Kayak use AI to help travelers find the best flight deals, suggest accommodations, and create personalized itineraries based on their preferences. These platforms analyze user behavior and travel trends to provide tailored recommendations, ensuring that every trip is optimized for budget, interests, and time.

For example, Google Trips automatically gathers information from your Gmail (like flight details and hotel reservations) and organizes it into a single itinerary, complete with maps, activity suggestions, and restaurant recommendations. The AI also alerts you if there are any changes to your flight status or other travel-related updates.

AI-powered tools can even suggest alternative routes or dates to help travelers save money. Platforms like Skyscanner use AI to predict price changes for flights, notifying users when prices are expected to rise or fall, allowing them to book at the best time.

9.2 AI in Transportation: Self-Driving Cars and Beyond

The development of self-driving cars represents one of the most exciting advancements in AI. Companies like Tesla, Waymo, and Uber are pioneering autonomous vehicles that use AI to navigate roads, avoid obstacles, and transport passengers safely. These cars rely on AI-powered sensors, cameras, and LIDAR systems to understand their surroundings and make real-time driving decisions.

In addition to self-driving cars, AI is also transforming public transportation. AI-powered routing systems optimize bus and train schedules based on real-time traffic conditions, improving efficiency and reducing wait times for passengers. This is particularly useful in densely populated cities where traffic congestion is a significant issue.

As AI continues to advance, it's likely that autonomous vehicles will become more common, and AI-driven transportation systems will reshape how we travel—making it safer, faster, and more sustainable.

9.3 AI-Powered Language Translation for Travelers

For travelers visiting foreign countries, language barriers can be a challenge. AI-powered language translation tools, like Google Translate and DeepL, are making it easier for travelers to communicate in different languages. These apps can translate text, speech, and even images in real-time, allowing users to navigate menus, signs, and conversations with ease.

Google Translate's conversation mode allows two people speaking different languages to have a real-time translated conversation. The AI listens to each speaker, translates the text, and speaks the translated version aloud, facilitating smooth communication between individuals who don't share a common language.

These AI translation tools are particularly useful for navigating foreign cities, ordering food, or asking for directions, making travel more accessible to a broader audience.

Chapter 10: Ethical Considerations and Challenges of AI

10.1 Privacy and Data Concerns with AI

One of the most pressing challenges of AI adoption in daily life is the issue of privacy. Many AI applications rely on large datasets that include sensitive personal information, such as location data, browsing history, and even biometric data. As AI becomes more integrated into everyday tasks—such as shopping, navigation, and personal productivity—the amount of personal data it processes increases exponentially.

Privacy concerns arise from how companies collect, store, and use this data. Platforms like Facebook, Google, and Amazon collect vast amounts of user data to train their AI algorithms, often without users fully understanding how their information is being used. This raises questions about data security and the potential misuse of personal information.

AI-driven systems also pose risks for data breaches, where sensitive information can be exposed to hackers or malicious entities. Furthermore, the increasing use of AI in surveillance, such as facial recognition technologies, adds another layer of concern regarding individuals' rights to privacy.

Consumers and regulators alike are calling for stricter data protection laws, transparency in how AI systems use data, and improved security measures to protect personal information.

10.2 AI and Job Automation: Navigating the Future of Work

One of the most hotly debated topics surrounding AI is its impact on jobs. As AI becomes more capable of performing tasks traditionally done by humans—such as customer service, manufacturing, and data analysis—there are growing concerns about job displacement. Automation is already affecting industries like retail, logistics, and manufacturing, where AI-powered robots and algorithms are replacing human workers.

However, AI is not only eliminating jobs but also creating new opportunities. As more businesses adopt AI, the demand for professionals skilled in AI development, data analysis, and AI management is growing. This shift is leading to the emergence of new job categories, such as AI trainers, data curators, and AI ethics consultants.

Navigating the future of work with AI requires individuals to upskill and reskill to stay relevant in an AI-driven economy. Governments and educational institutions are also exploring ways to adapt to these changes by offering programs and training in AI-related fields.

10.3 The Ethical Implications of AI in Decision-Making

AI is increasingly being used to make decisions in areas such as finance, healthcare, hiring, and law enforcement. While these systems can provide efficiency and accuracy, they also raise ethical concerns, particularly when it comes to bias and fairness.

AI systems are only as good as the data they are trained on. If the training data reflects historical biases, the AI can replicate and even amplify those biases. For example, in hiring processes, AI algorithms might favor candidates from certain demographics if the training data reflects biased hiring practices. In law enforcement, predictive policing algorithms can unfairly target communities of color if they are trained on biased crime data.

These ethical implications have sparked debates about how to ensure that AI systems make fair and unbiased decisions. Companies and governments are beginning to implement ethical AI guidelines, requiring transparency in AI decision-making and mandating audits to identify and eliminate biases in algorithms.

10.4 AI and Bias: Addressing Systemic Issues in AI Algorithms

Bias in AI is one of the most significant challenges facing the technology today. AI algorithms can unintentionally reinforce harmful stereotypes and discriminatory practices if they are trained on biased data. This issue has been observed in areas such as facial recognition, where AI systems have shown higher error rates in recognizing people of color compared to white individuals.

Efforts to combat bias in AI include improving the diversity of data used to train algorithms and creating more transparent AI systems that allow for greater scrutiny of how decisions are made. AI researchers are also exploring ways to build fairness and ethical considerations directly into the development process, ensuring that systems are designed with inclusivity in mind.

At the same time, there is a growing recognition that addressing bias in AI requires collaboration between technologists, ethicists, and policymakers. By ensuring that diverse voices are involved in the development of AI systems, we can help reduce bias and create more equitable outcomes.

10.5 Balancing Innovation and Responsibility in AI

AI is advancing rapidly, offering new opportunities for innovation in fields like healthcare, education, and transportation. However, with these advancements come responsibilities. As AI becomes more integrated into everyday life, it is crucial to balance innovation with ethical considerations, ensuring that AI is used in ways that benefit society as a whole.

For companies developing AI technologies, this means implementing ethical guidelines and engaging in responsible AI development. It also involves ensuring that AI systems are transparent, explainable, and accountable. Users of AI systems—whether individuals or organizations—must also be mindful of how they use AI, considering its potential impact on privacy, fairness, and society at large.

Governments and regulatory bodies play a critical role in ensuring that AI is developed and deployed responsibly. This includes creating legal frameworks that address privacy concerns, data protection, and the ethical use of AI, while also fostering innovation and technological progress.

In the long term, the goal is to create AI systems that are trustworthy, ethical, and aligned with human values.

Chapter 11: Getting Started with AI

11.1 Easy Steps to Integrate AI into Your Daily Routine

AI may sound intimidating to those unfamiliar with the technology, but integrating AI into your daily routine is easier than you might think. Many AI-powered tools are designed for everyday users, offering simple, intuitive interfaces that require no technical expertise.

Here are a few steps to start using AI in your daily life:

Begin with a Virtual Assistant: If you're not already using one, virtual assistants like Google Assistant, Amazon Alexa, or Apple's Siri are excellent introductions to AI. These voice-controlled assistants can help you set reminders, play music, control smart home devices, and even answer questions about the weather or news.

Use AI-Powered Apps: Apps like Grammarly for writing assistance, Todoist for task management, and Fitbod for personalized fitness plans use AI to help you improve productivity, health, and efficiency. Start exploring these tools and integrate them into your routine.

Set Up a Smart Home: Consider adding AI-powered devices to your home, like a Nest Thermostat, Ring doorbell, or smart lighting systems. These devices can automate tasks like adjusting the temperature, controlling lights, and managing home security, making your life more convenient and efficient.

Explore AI in Entertainment: Platforms like Spotify, Netflix, and YouTube already use AI to recommend personalized content. Engage with these features by rating content, following recommendations, and allowing the AI to learn more about your preferences.

11.2 Popular AI Tools and Apps for Beginners

There are countless AI-powered tools available for everyday users. Here are some of the most popular AI tools and apps that can help you get started:

Grammarly: An AI-powered writing assistant that checks for grammar, punctuation, and style errors.

Todoist: A task management app that uses AI to help prioritize tasks and manage deadlines.

Fitbod: A fitness app that creates personalized workout plans based on your goals and progress.

Google Assistant: A virtual assistant that helps with scheduling, reminders, and managing smart home devices.

Amazon Alexa: A voice-controlled assistant that can play music, control smart devices, and provide information.

IFTTT: An automation app that allows you to connect different services and automate repetitive tasks.

Google Photos: Uses AI to organize, tag, and enhance your photos, making it easier to manage your digital library.

11.3 Customizing AI Solutions for Your Needs

One of the biggest advantages of AI is its ability to adapt to your specific needs and preferences. Whether you're using AI for work, home automation, or personal development, there are numerous ways to customize these tools for maximum benefit.

For example, in Google Assistant, you can set up routines to automate tasks based on time or location. A morning routine might include turning on lights, adjusting the thermostat, and reading the day's news, while an evening routine could involve dimming the lights and playing relaxing music.

In productivity apps like Todoist, you can use AI to prioritize tasks based on urgency and deadlines. The AI learns from how you complete tasks and adapts its suggestions to better fit your workflow.

By exploring the customization options in AI-powered tools, you can create solutions that make your life more efficient, personalized, and enjoyable.

11.4 Overcoming AI Fatigue: Knowing When to Disconnect

While AI offers numerous benefits, it's essential to recognize when it's time to disconnect and avoid over-reliance on technology. AI fatigue can occur when individuals feel overwhelmed by the constant presence of AI in their daily lives, particularly when it comes to managing notifications, tasks, or interactions with virtual assistants.

To prevent AI fatigue, it's important to:

Set Boundaries: Limit the number of notifications you receive from AI-powered tools. Most apps allow you to customize notification settings to avoid being bombarded with constant updates.

Take Breaks from Tech: Set aside time each day to disconnect from AI-driven devices and apps. Use this time for activities like reading, walking, or engaging in creative pursuits.

Be Mindful of AI Use: Use AI tools selectively, focusing on those that add genuine value to your life. Avoid becoming overly dependent on AI for tasks that can be done without technology.

By using AI mindfully, you can enjoy its benefits without feeling overwhelmed.

11.5 Preparing for the AI-Driven Future

As AI continues to evolve, its role in our daily lives will only expand. To stay ahead of the curve, it's important to stay informed about new developments in AI and be open to exploring new tools and technologies. Regularly updating your skills, especially in areas like digital literacy and data privacy, will ensure that you can leverage AI to your advantage.

AI is shaping the future of work, education, health, and entertainment. By embracing these changes and adapting to them, you'll be well-prepared to thrive in an AI-driven world.

Chapter 12: Conclusion: Embrace AI for a Smarter Future

12.1 Recap of AI's Role in Improving Life

Throughout this eBook, we've explored the many ways in which AI is transforming daily life—from automating repetitive tasks and improving productivity to revolutionizing industries like healthcare, finance, and entertainment. AI has become a powerful tool that can enhance our lives in countless ways, making everyday tasks more efficient, personalized, and convenient.

12.2 Encouraging Responsible Use of AI

As we embrace the benefits of AI, it's crucial to use this technology responsibly. This means being mindful of privacy, ensuring ethical AI development, and staying aware of how AI systems collect and use data. By fostering a balance between innovation and responsibility, we can ensure that AI continues to serve the greater good while respecting individual rights.

12.3 Final Thoughts on Staying Ahead of the Curve with AI Innovation

AI is here to stay, and its influence on our lives will only grow in the coming years. By staying informed, adapting to new technologies, and using AI tools that align with your goals and values, you can continue to benefit from the advancements in AI. Embrace the opportunities AI presents, and remain open to learning and evolving alongside this transformative technology.

The future is bright, and with AI as a partner in daily life, we can create a smarter, more efficient, and more personalized world.

Disclaimer:

This eBook was created with the assistance of Artificial Intelligence (AI). The information provided in this book is for informational purposes only and is intended to offer general guidance on the topics discussed. While efforts have been made to ensure the accuracy and relevance of the content, the authors and AI systems involved in its creation make no guarantees or warranties regarding the completeness, timeliness, or suitability of the information for any particular purpose. Readers are encouraged to seek professional advice or conduct further research where necessary. The use of this eBook is at your own discretion and risk.

www.ingramcontent.com/pod-product-compliance
Lightning Source LLC
Chambersburg PA
CBHW081021240526
45471CB00018B/3935